Celebrate Colossians

participant guide

wesleyan
publishing
house

Indianapolis, Indiana

Copyright © 2008 by Wesleyan Publishing House
Published by Wesleyan Publishing House
Indianapolis, Indiana 46250
Printed in the United States of America
ISBN: 978-0-89827-391-5

Contents

Celebrate Series Overview

This *Celebrate* DVD and participant guide is part of a series of studies aimed at helping participants study and apply God's word and experience life transformation. Lessons are designed to be used in small groups but can easily be adapted for individual study.

The DVDs in this series feature the Bible teaching of Pastor Keith Loy. In each study, Pastor Loy will walk you through a book or books from the Bible, with a focus on helping participants apply what they learn in a practical way.

Each participant guide contains study notes, as well as additional material to help participants process and apply the teaching on the DVD. These include ideas for group sharing, connecting, and discussing, as well as action steps participants can follow to implement their learning. You'll also find helpful instructions and guidelines for those who are facilitating small groups.

As you *Celebrate* and study the Word, whether as an individual or in a group, may God richly bless your life and help you grow in knowledge and obedience to our Lord Jesus Christ.

Study Preview

Rarely does a person encounter the life-transforming story of Jesus and walk away uninspired or unimpressed. In fact, Jesus is almost universally regarded as one of the greatest spiritual leaders of all time, a person to be admired and respected, discussed and emulated. Unfortunately, even though such admiration is well intended, it still falls far short of recognizing the unique character and contribution of Jesus. For he is

> The image of the invisible God, the firstborn over all creation. For by him all things were created: things in heaven and on earth, visible and invisible, whether thrones or powers or rulers or authorities; all things were created by him and for him. He is before all things, and in him all things hold together. And he is the head of the body, the church; he is the beginning and the firstborn from among the dead, so that in everything he might have the supremacy (Col. 1:15–18).

Too often, Jesus is treated as one man among many—worthy of respect, but not worship; honor, but not submission. In such a time, it can be challenging for Christians to remain convinced about Jesus in their own minds and to courageously assert the truth in the presence of those who don't believe.

Paul wrote the words quoted above to the Christians at Colosse because they were facing a very similar challenge. The Roman world was filled with "deities," and some people simply added Jesus to the list. Others knew just enough about Jesus to be dangerous, and they spread false teachings about Jesus, even among the churches! Paul's primary message to the Colossian Christians was to "continue in your faith, established and firm, not moved from the hope held out in the gospel" (Col. 1:23), a message that is just as timely and relevant for believers today.

In this DVD study on Colossians, you will be

- strengthened in your faith in Jesus to comprehend his uniqueness,

- encouraged in your walk with Jesus to experience the fullness of Christ, and

- challenged in your service to Jesus to "work at it with all your heart" (Col. 3:23).

As you work your way through these twelve lessons individually or as a group, may God "fill you with the knowledge of his will through all spiritual wisdom and understanding" (Col. 1:9). Amen.

Guidelines for Group Facilitators

This DVD Bible study is designed as a *plug-and-play* small group experience, with little or no preparation necessary prior to each session. However, you'll find it helpful for your group to have a facilitator, someone who will manage details and guide the group's experience. Here are some helpful tips for those who serve as group facilitators.

SET THE ATMOSPHERE

Small groups should be casual, welcoming, and inclusive. Arrange a meeting place where people will feel comfortable and relaxed. Most often, this will be a group member's home, but it could also be a room in your church building that is specially equipped for this kind of meeting. Providing coffee, other beverages, and snacks can also contribute to a relaxed atmosphere.

ENCOURAGE PARTICIPATION

Make sure everyone has the opportunity to participate fully in your group. Invite different people to pray or read or provide refreshments. Also, be ready to give instructions like "This time let's hear from someone who hasn't spoken up yet" or "Jason, I'm wondering what you're thinking about this. Anything you'd like to share?"

KEEP ON SCHEDULE

This DVD Bible study is designed to take no more than ninety minutes for each session. Here is a typical schedule:

Welcome and Prayer	5 minutes
Share	10 minutes
Connect	15–20 minutes
Discover	10 minutes
Discuss	25–30 minutes
Implement	5–10 minutes
Wrap Up	5 minutes

As facilitator, guide your group through each step of the process and make sure they stay on track and on schedule.

Try to keep your meetings as positive as possible. Establish ground rules early on so that each person in your group is treated with kindness and respect.

Being a group facilitator does require a bit of extra time, but your servant leadership can make a big difference in the overall experience of the group.

The Believer's Identity in Christ

COLOSSIANS 1:1–3

WELCOME and PRAYER
(5 minutes)

SHARE
(10 minutes)

Take turns sharing what you hope to gain from this experience.

CONNECT
(15–20 minutes)

Dew glistened on colorful canopies shading merchants' wares as the sun peeked above the hills in the east. A man in beggar's clothes stepped near a produce cart just as a basket toppled off, spilling fruit at his feet. Quickly, he began to help gather up the fruit, when suddenly the owner of the cart struck him with a stick. Unfazed, the beggar went back to gathering the fruit until the owner struck him again. With this blow, the beggar's tunic parted just enough to reveal the royal signet ring hanging from his necklace. With horror, the merchant understood that this beggar was no bum, but royalty in disguise.

Knowing a person's true identity can change everything. Knowing your own identity in Christ will transform your life.

Facilitator: Lead the group to participate in one or both of the following activities.

1. Play Twenty Questions. Have one person write down the name of a famous person—one others will definitely know. Then take turns asking simple yes-or-no questions until someone is able to guess the name of the famous person.

2. Take turns completing the following sentence: "My favorite story about mistaken identity is . . ."

DISCOVER
(10 minutes)

Complete the study notes as you watch the DVD together.

Ever since the fall in the garden, mankind has been trying to explain and discover ___God___.

Four types of attempts to explain God are religious, ___Religious___, ___Islam___, and ___Scientology___.

Emotional
Intellectual/regular
Rules/legalism
Sacred fear of up things

10

The three cities, _Pedoven_, _Hyrolop_, and _Colossa_, were in the Lycus River valley.

Collesse had been a key meeting place for East and West trade and a center for new thought.

Paul understood his _identity_ in Christ.

Apostle means *one who is sent* or *ambassador*.

Being a Christian is not _life style_; it is a _24|7_.

The distinguishing mark for Christians is that God has _chosen_ them.

Paul calls the Christians in Colosse _Saints_.

Colosse, located in modern-day Turkey, became a center for Gnosticism, a mixture of Christian thought, Greek philosophy, and mysticism. Gnosticism denied that Jesus was born in human flesh and taught people to seek salvation through initiation into a secret, hidden knowledge of Christ. The heresy Paul argued against in this letter may have been an early form of Gnosticism.

A saint is one who is _set apart_ or _dedicate_ to God.

If we don't realize _who_ we are in Christ, it is almost impossible for us to live out _what is_ we are in Christ. We are a _first pairts_, an _heir_ to the kingdom.

The second thing Paul did in the opening of his letter was to
_____.

> Today we use the word saint *to describe a super-Christian, such as the apostle Paul or Mother Teresa, or someone who has just performed a good and selfless act: "Oh, she is a saint!" For Paul, all Christians are saints. Not that he devalued the word* saint; *instead he recognized that all Christians have a special status. The word means* set apart *or* dedicated to God.

People don't care how much you _know_, until they know much you _care_.

Only the _greatful_ and _appreclify_ leader can draw the best out of those whom he or she leads.

Paul _understood_ his identity, _valued_ the community, and _called_ them to responsibility.

DISCUSS
(25–30 minutes)

1. Why do you think people have such a deep desire to know and explain God?

2. What are some false ways you or those around you have tried to explain God?

3. Pastor Loy listed four misguided attempts to explain God. Which one do you most often struggle with? For what reasons?

4. How would you define a believer's true identity in Christ? How does knowing one's identity in Christ change a person's life?

5. In what ways are all Christians called to be apostles?

6. What does it mean to be chosen by God?

7. In what ways can we respond to the calling of God?

8. When you think of sainthood, who or what comes to mind?

IMPLEMENT
(5–10 minutes)

Choose at least one activity to do before the next session. Tell one other person which item you chose.

1. Write out your answer to this question: What do you think is your true identity in Christ? Write first about the identity all Christians share and then specifically about the person God created you to be.

The Greek word for apostle, apostolos, refers to one who is sent out with an official message or as an envoy or ambassador to a new region. The apostle of Jesus Christ, in proclaiming the message of Jesus, exercises the authority of Jesus.

2. Seek feedback from others about how well you are living out your true identity in Christ. Identify areas where you can grow.

3. Develop a plan for growth in living out your identity in Christ. Be very specific about how you would like to change. For example, instead of saying, "I want to be more compassionate when others are hurting," say, "When others are hurting, I will take time to listen and empathize."

4. Write a letter or E-mail to someone who needs encouragement this week.

WRAP UP
(5 minutes)

In the next lesson Pastor Loy will explore Paul's prayer for the church at Colosse that they may "live a life worthy of the Lord and may please him in every way: bearing fruit in every good work." As you look ahead to next week's lesson, meditate on what it means for Christians to bear fruit in every good work.

What Fruit Do You Bear?

COLOSSIANS 1:4–14

WELCOME and PRAYER
(5 minutes)

SHARE
(10 minutes)

Take turns sharing what you learned from applying the last session.

CONNECT
(15–20 minutes)

At the center of every fruit tree is a *fruit line*. The sap running in this line determines the type of fruit the tree will produce. A tree will *only* produce the kind of fruit that naturally develops from this source. A Macintosh apple tree will always produce Macintosh apples. A Valencia orange tree will only produce Valencia oranges. If you want to know what kind of tree you have, it's not necessary to cut it open and test the sap. You can judge it by its fruit.

The revolutionary change that God achieves deep inside our hearts will be revealed to others by the kind and quality of fruit we produce in our lives. What does your fruit say about you?

Facilitator: Lead the group to participate in the following discussion.

Both Jesus and Paul use the image of bearing fruit to illustrate the change that takes place in a Christian's life post-conversion. Discuss why you think fruit-bearing is such a key analogy in the New Testament to illustrate the transformed life of a believer. What additional analogies can you think of that might effectively communicate the same truth in today's culture?

DISCOVER
(10 minutes)

Complete the study notes as you watch the DVD together.

Paul's summary of the Christian life is _____, _____, and _____.

_____ is the beginning of our walk with Christ.

_____ is Christianity lived out.

It is impossible to have __faith__ in God without __loving__ people.

Colossians 1:4–14

When you have faith in Jesus Christ, it is always _____ in _____ toward others.

Hope is the ground or very foundation on which faith and love rest.

Faith is our _____ relationship with God. Love is our _____ relationships with others. Hope is the _____ of the two.

Epaphras (verse 7) was a disciple of Paul who founded the church in Colosse. He communicated with Paul while Paul was in prison and kept him up-to-date about what was happening with the community of believers. This helped Paul know what topics to address when he wrote to them.

God designed the Christian life to be a life of _____.
It is a call to _action_.

Paul gives us two key identifiers of real Christianity: (1) a changed _life_ and (2) a changed _heart_.

When a person gives their heart to Christ, _everything_ is different.

Fruit production is the second key identifier for a Christian.

The fruit of a Christian is to _love others_

obedience is the key to fruit production.

17

If we want to have more fruit-producing faith, then we must have a bigger view of _God_.

True faith inspires _____, love _____ it, and hope _____ it.

A _____ faith is the very thing that God planned for the Christian.

_____ is the fuel that drives faith and love.

DISCUSS
(25–30 minutes)

1. Why are faith, hope, and love such key elements of the Christian life?

2. What is the difference between a changed heart and a changed life? Can you have one without the other?

3. Paul defined the fruit of the Spirit as love, joy, peace, patience, kindness, goodness, faithfulness, gentleness, and self-control. Which of these characteristics are fruit of a changed heart and which are characteristics of a changed life? Why?

4. Why do you think Paul considered love to be greater than faith and hope?

5. When God changes your heart, how is your life changed?

✗ 6. What role does the Holy Spirit play in the process of changing your heart and life?

7. Why does faith need to be accompanied by action?

8. How does hope fuel us in our Christian walk?

> The word fruit refers figuratively to the various types of evidence in a person's life that he or she has been genuinely transformed by God. At the time Paul wrote Colossians, the church was growing and producing new converts almost daily. That's one kind of fruit. Another kind is what Paul called the fruit of the Spirit in Galatians 5:22–23.

IMPLEMENT
(5–10 minutes)

Choose at least one activity to do before the next session. Tell one other person which item you chose.

1. Of the three key characteristics of a Christian—faith, hope, and love—which are you having the most success with? Which are you having the least success with? Develop a plan for strengthening the characteristic you are wrestling with most.

2. Make a list of the types of fruit you produced before your heart was changed by God. Then compare it with a list of the fruit God now produces in and through you. What did you learn about yourself from this exercise?

The dominion of darkness Paul referred to in verse 13 is the destructive power Satan and sin hold over the world. This power can only be broken by the power and authority of Christ. Christians are rescued from the kingdom of darkness and delivered into the kingdom of Jesus.

3. Orchards continually need to be pruned and cared for. Make a list of ways you can take care of yourself spiritually to ensure good fruit production.

4. Memorize the fruit of the Spirit listed in Galatians 5:22–23.

WRAP UP
(5 minutes)

In the next lesson Pastor Loy will be discussing the supremacy of Jesus Christ. There is no one like him, and we are completely and utterly lost without him. What's even more surprising is that he loves us unconditionally and wants us have new life in him.

The Supremacy of Christ

COLOSSIANS 1:15–23

WELCOME and PRAYER
(5 minutes)

SHARE
(10 minutes)

Take turns sharing what you learned from applying the last session.

CONNECT
(15–20 minutes)

The villagers swarmed around the missionaries. They were fascinated by all of the gadgets and electronic instruments the missionaries had brought with them. But they were most astonished at a small piece of glass that one of the missionaries had pulled out of her bag. They were amazed because, looking into this piece of glass, they could see images— reflections of themselves. Many of the villagers saw their own likeness for the first time that day.

Jesus is the visible image of the invisible God, and his image is to be reflected in us. Many people will first glimpse Jesus through the reflection they see in our lives.

Facilitator: Lead the group to participate in the following discussion.

Discuss as a group what it means for Jesus to be the supreme ruler. Make a list of every realm you think Jesus is actively ruling over. Is he ruling over the Church? Is he ruling over the universe? Is he ruling over democratic nations such as the United States? What about nations that are run by monarchs, dictators, or religious leaders? What, if anything, does it mean for Jesus to be ruler in each of these areas?

DISCOVER
(10 minutes)

Complete the study notes as you watch the DVD together.

The term *image* means that which _____ an object.

God has a reflection. His name is _____.

Christ is the _____ of who and what _____ is.

The "before" in Colossians 1:17 does not mean Jesus was _____.

Jesus was never a part of creation; he is the _____.

It's no wonder that the winds and waves _____ him; he _____ them.

For centuries Greek philosophers taught that everything needed a _____ cause.

> The firstborn over all creation. Early in the Church's history, a misunderstanding of this phrase led to confusion and disagreement over the identity of Jesus Christ. Some thought that it meant Jesus was created by God. In reality, the phrase is an analogy, comparing Jesus' status to the status of the first-born son, the heir.

Paul insists that the primary cause is _____.

We can be so _____ that we think creation is about _____. That's _____.

"All _____ is incomprehensible without Christ."
—Renan

God created _____ that man has ever seen—for his own _____.

Jesus Christ has taken care of _____ things.

Jesus Christ is _____ that we _____.

Jesus Christ must be _____ in _____.

Jesus has brought _____ into the presence of God.

You are _____ and _____ as you stand before God because of Jesus Christ.

The _____ of God's plan was birthed in Jesus Christ.

Faith requires _____, and action first begins with _____.

DISCUSS
(25–30 minutes)

1. Pastor Loy mentioned that people want the real thing when they search for God. What do you think they are searching for?

2. What are some counterfeit forms of God that people search for?

3. In what ways does Jesus' existence on earth validate God's existence?

4. What different roles do you think Jesus and God the Father played in creation?

5. Why is it so easy for human beings to put themselves at the center of the universe?

6. Why do you think God created flowers that no one may ever see?

> Firstborn among the dead. Jesus was already the firstborn over all creation (1:15). Through his death and resurrection, Jesus became the firstborn among the new creation.

7. Since creation is not about us, why do you think God took the time to create us and then to save us?

8. What are ways you can make sure Jesus is the Head of your life? Your church?

IMPLEMENT
(5–10 minutes)

Choose at least one activity to do before the next session. Tell one other person which item you chose.

1. Examine your life to see if Christ is truly supreme in all areas. Journal your reflections and share them with a close friend.

2. As you gather with other Christians, be intentional about making Christ the Head of your gatherings. Create a visual reminder that he is on the throne and we are not.

> *He is the head of the body, the Church. Jesus Christ ultimately will be seen as the Lord of all, even by those who have rejected him. If he is their Lord, certainly he stands as Lord over his Church, those he has redeemed, those who honor him as Savior and King.*

3. Discuss with at least one other person the idea that all of creation was created by God and for God. How should that truth make a practical difference in our lives?

4. Memorize Colossians 1:15–16. Start each day this week by reading or reciting those verses and contemplating the supremacy of Christ.

WRAP UP
(5 minutes)

In the next lesson Pastor Loy will be exploring what it means to be grounded in Christ and to have our feet firmly planted in the Word of God. After reviewing the passage from today's lesson, prepare for next week by meditating on Colossians 2:1–7.

Grounded in Christ

COLOSSIANS 2:1–7

WELCOME and PRAYER
(5 minutes)

SHARE
(10 minutes)

Take turns sharing what you learned from applying the last session.

CONNECT
(15–20 minutes)

The desert landscape of the southwestern United States is a harsh environment that sustains life, especially vegetation, only with difficulty. In this arid climate where most trees can't survive, one type of tree has managed to thrive and become one of the oldest species of trees on the planet—the Joshua tree. The Joshua tree is equipped to survive its parched surroundings because its root system grows very complex and very deep, sometimes stretching for miles to find a source of water.

How deep are your roots in Christ? How well could your Christian life sustain the harsh environment of a desert period?

Facilitator: Lead the group to participate in the following discussion.

Many people are very interested in genealogy and spend a lot of time tracing out their family trees. Others have a strong sense of their family's cultural or ethnic heritage. Take turns talking about what importance group members place on their family history and how knowing (or not knowing) their genealogy or heritage has affected their lives. Discuss the importance of family history and how our roots provide context and stability for our lives.

DISCOVER
(10 minutes)

Complete the study notes as you watch the DVD together.

If we want to grow in the greatness of God, we must discover the _____ of God.

If we are to grow deeper in Christ, we must _____ deeper in Christ.

Great _____ and a strong _____ makes the soul _____.

Paul wants his readers to have a faith that is built on the _____ of Christ that will strengthen their _____ of Christ and result in _____ to all.

You do not fit the _____ into your life; you fit your _____ into the Word of God.

Laodicea was a neighboring town to Colosse on the Lycus River valley. The church at Laodicea later received one of the seven letters in the book of Revelation and was harshly rebuked by Jesus for being lukewarm in their devotion to Christ and his kingdom.

Our testimony of Christ must be built upon a _____ of Christ.

Freedom in Christ requires a _____ of Christ, and this comes from being in the _____.

Christianity is more than just _____ knowledge. It is a _____, a _____, a day-to-day _____ with the Lord.

Christians should be deeply _____ in Christ.

We need to water and fertilize by _____, _____, and having _____ with God.

When we trust Jesus to save us, we are set on the right _____.

The unfailing mark of a healthy spiritual life is _____.

We should never fail to express _____ for the new _____, the new _____ that we have found in Jesus Christ.

Positive _____ always accelerates learning.

DISCUSS
(25–30 minutes)

1. What does it mean to be grounded in God's Word?

2. How does a person go about being grounded in Jesus Christ and his Word?

3. What challenges do Christians face in grounding themselves in God's Word?

> *The mystery Paul alluded to in this first part of his letter is the fact that God has chosen to bring salvation to all the world, not just to Israel, through his Son Jesus Christ.*

4. What has helped you experience success in building a strong foundation on God's Word?

5. What is the difference between head knowledge of God and heart knowledge of him?

6. Why is it important for us to continue to grow in both head knowledge and heart knowledge?

7. Why is gratitude such a key element in Christian living and for growing in Christ?

8. How is serving others an expression of our gratitude?

> To be able to withstand the fine-sounding arguments of the world, the Christian must be deeply rooted in the knowledge and wisdom of God.

IMPLEMENT
(5–10 minutes)

Choose at least one activity to do before the next session. Tell one other person which item you chose.

1. Take a head knowledge versus heart knowledge survey. Make a list of what you believe to be true of Christ. Then try to describe specifically how each belief shapes your life and actions. Where might your beliefs need to be better reflected in your actions?

2. Choose and commit to a regular plan of reading and meditating on Scripture. Create practical applications of the passages you study.

3. Each day for a week, choose one person to be the recipient of your gratitude. In gratefulness for God's work in your life, make a difference in each person's life by sending a note of encouragement, meeting a specific need, or telling the person how he or she has impacted you.

WRAP UP
(5 minutes)

In the next lesson Pastor Loy will be teaching about Christian freedom. What does it mean to be free in Christ? What are we free from? How far does our freedom extend? And most importantly, how does our freedom in Christ help us serve and love others? To get a jump start, read Colossians 2:8–15.

True Freedom in Christ

COLOSSIANS 2:8–15

WELCOME and PRAYER
(5 minutes)

SHARE
(10 minutes)

*Take turns sharing what you learned
from applying the last session.*

CONNECT
(15–20 minutes)

Walking through the archway and hearing the gate slam shut behind him one last time, he still felt apprehension and anxiety. Only this time it was focused on what lay beyond the walls of the prison instead of inside them. For the first time in twenty years he was totally and completely free. Well, almost. There were still the check-ins with his parole officer. And he had to be careful not to violate the terms of his parole and thus find his way back to prison. But still, he was free, finally free, to experience life to its fullest.

Paul and other biblical authors described salvation as rescue, deliverance, liberation, and freedom from bondage. Freedom with responsibility, but freedom nonetheless.

Facilitator: Lead the group to participate in the following discussion.

Share stories or personal experiences about being trapped, either physically or emotionally. Talk about the thoughts and feelings you experience at three different stages: (1) when you first realize you're trapped, (2) when you begin to lose hope, and (3) when you know for certain that help is on the way. How does it feel when you finally regain freedom?

DISCOVER
(10 minutes)

Complete the study notes as you watch the DVD together.

False teachers were trying to impress rules, rituals, and regulations on the Colossian Christians as their source of

_____.

There is a difference between being _____ something and being _____ something.

The discovery of _____ begins in the discovery of

_____.

The five things we have in Christ are _____,
_____, _____, _____, and
_____.

Everyone who has accepted Christ
shares in his _____.

Spiritual growth doesn't come by
_____, but by _____.
We grow from the _____, not
from _____.

> The church in Colosse was probably dealing with the false philosophies of early Gnosticism, as well as legalism. Gnosticism asserted that salvation occurred through perfect knowledge, and legalism asserted that salvation occurred through perfect behavior.

Spiritual _____ comes when
we try to work for God instead of work out for God.

Through Christ's death we are made free from our
_____ self.

Many Christians are still _____ by the _____,
but God wants us to be _____.

God's grace is _____ favor, and it comes to us free
of _____.

If there's anything the church needs to express more, it's
_____.

There's nothing we can do to make God love us _____ or _____.

God makes us _____ with Christ and forgives all our _____.

God hates _____ enough that he showers us with _____.

DISCUSS
(25–30 minutes)

1. What prominent false philosophies cause the modern church problems, as first-century false belief systems affected the Colossian church?

2. How should a Christian combat false philosophies and views?

> Paul taught that the physical act of circumcision from the Old Testament law is no longer required for believers, but it is still necessary for spiritual circumcision to take place. Circumcision of the heart is what God has always truly desired. The physical act was a symbol of the spiritual reality.

3. In what ways did Christ possess in bodily form all the fullness of God?

4. What does it mean for us that in Christ we have been given fullness?

5. What is true freedom in Christ?

6. Why is it hard for people to accept the unconditional grace and love of God?

7. Is truly unconditional love possible between people?

8. In what ways is Jesus the foundation for all Christians?

> Paul's image of Christ nailing the rules and regulations of the law to the cross was a powerful way of proclaiming that Jesus fulfilled all those requirements through his sinless life and sacrificial death on the cross, securing freedom for every believer.

IMPLEMENT
(5–10 minutes)

Choose at least one activity to do before the next session. Tell one other person which item you chose.

1. Examine your heart to see if there are rules and regulations you hold as true that are not in line with God's Word.

2. Be on the lookout for any false philosophies that are presented to you throughout the upcoming week—through the media or another person. Create a list of such philosophies and share them with the group at your next meeting.

3. If you feel constricted in the Christian life, make a list of steps you can take to really experience the freedom Christ died to give you.

4. Continue to dig your roots deeper into the Word of God by committing to read his Word every day this next week.

WRAP UP
(5 minutes)

In the next lesson Pastor Loy will be discussing legalism and other pitfalls experienced by the Pharisees and other religious leaders of Paul's time. Sadly legalism is still a major problem for the church. The study passage for next time is Colossians 2:16–23.

Freedom from Legalism

COLOSSIANS 2:16–23

WELCOME and PRAYER
(5 minutes)

SHARE
(10 minutes)

Take turns sharing what you learned from applying the last session.

CONNECT
(15–20 minutes)

The room was a bright, blinding white. He stood there in line with the others, staring at the celestial surroundings. When it came his turn to stand before the throne, he pulled out a long, extensive list of the good deeds he had done. With a self-satisfied smirk he presented them to the judge. But the judge returned a blank stare, as one would look at a stranger. The list had seemed to show that they were very close friends, but the judge had no recollection of ever meeting the man.

When your life comes to an end, are you going to show God a list of all your good deeds? Or will you simply trust in the life, death, and resurrection of Jesus, as your Father lovingly accepts you, his child, into his arms?

Facilitator: Lead the group to participate in the following discussion.

People have different attitudes and opinions about rules, whether in playing a game or another area of life. Discuss with the group your answers to this question: Which of the following best describes your approach to rules?

- I follow all the rules all the time.
- I consider rules to be helpful suggestions or guidelines.
- I think rules are made to be broken.

Explain why you chose the answer you did.

DISCOVER
(10 minutes)

Complete the study notes as you watch the DVD together.

A sign can be for _____, _____, or _____, but a sign serves no purpose if you do not adhere to its _____.

Man's nature thrives on religious _____. Doing good for God is our _____ but not our _____. Our identity is found in _____.

Doing good religious deeds can inflate our _____.

Christians live under _____ not under _____.

When we add extra rules to our relationship with God, we are saying that Jesus isn't _____ for us.

Legalism is _____.

According to Old Testament law, certain foods were considered _____ or _____.

Jesus looks at the _____.

Christians are called to live by the _____.

Legalism is popular because people can _____ their own spiritual life by what they _____. Legalism causes people to _____ about their good deeds.

There are _____ awaiting the Christians who love God.

The term Paul used for the law, written code, was a business term. It means a bond or an IOU. Paul was teaching that the law revealed a debt all people had to pay. Jesus paid that debt on the cross and therefore fulfilled the law.

Trying to reach God through anyone or anything but _____ is idolatry.

Jesus Christ _____ is our mediator between God and man.

True spiritual maturity is learning to love like _____.
Such love requires that we _____ with others.

We _____ each other.

DISCUSS
(25–30 minutes)

1. In the Gospel of Luke, Jesus used yeast as an image of the Pharisees' sin. How is legalism like yeast?

2. Why does legalism constrict true growth in Christ?

3. How can Christians do good deeds and not fall prey to spiritual pride?

4. Why is it so important to remain connected to Jesus as the Head of the Church?

Christ not only fulfilled the law by his death. He conquered the devil and his cohorts and disarmed them from having any power against his chosen ones.

5. Why do you think Jesus battled so vigorously against legalism?

6. In what ways did Jesus fulfill the Old Testament law?

7. If the law has been fulfilled, what are God's commands for us today?

> Jesus Christ is the Head of the Church, and any time in history when the Church has gotten into trouble, it has been because it has tried to operate without its Head in the proper place.

8. Discuss what rules exist for holy living.

9. Some rules seem helpful even though they didn't come directly from the Bible. What should our attitude be toward such rules?

IMPLEMENT
(5–10 minutes)

Choose at least one activity to do before the next session. Tell one other person which item you chose.

1. Many churches still struggle with legalism. Journal your thoughts about the following questions: Where would rate your church in the area of legalism on scale of 1 to 10 (1 = extreme legalism; 10 = completely free in Christ)? How does your church best express its freedom in Christ? Where does it need help expressing its freedom in Christ?

2. Rate yourself on the legalism scale described in question 1; then write down your answers to the following questions: How do you feel about your own freedom in Christ? Do you tend more toward legalism or lawlessness? What do you need to do to curb your tendencies?

3. Identify areas in your life where you might be holding yourself or others to a different standard than Scripture. Ask God to help you have the proper attitude about such guidelines.

WRAP UP
(5 minutes)

In the next lesson, Pastor Loy will be discussing holiness and holy living. Since this is a central doctrine for The Wesleyan Church, do some homework this week: Look up the Wesleyan view of holiness. Also, begin to study Colossians 3:1–9.

Holy Living Today

COLOSSIANS 3:1–9

WELCOME and PRAYER
(5 minutes)

SHARE
(10 minutes)

*Take turns sharing what you learned
from applying the last session.*

CONNECT
(15–20 minutes)

Ten-year-old Sarah had just been accepted into a
private school on a scholarship. As she looked
over the school's dress code, she knew that her
clothes did not match up and would stand out. On
Sarah's first day, despite her putting together as
nice an outfit she could, the other kids still pointed
her out and laughed at her. One mother, picking
up her child at the end of the day, overheard some
of the taunting. That evening, she quietly left a
brand-new outfit on Sarah's doorstep. The next

day Sarah proudly walked through school in her new clothes.

A new set of clothes, seemingly insignificant, can do wonders for a person's self-confidence. Imagine the difference when a new believer exchanges sin-stained rags for the robe of Christ.

Facilitator: Lead the group to participate in the following discussion.

In the last two lessons, Paul strongly condemned legalism and the false holiness it produces. The title of the study passage in the NIV for today's lesson is "Rules for Holy Living." Discuss the dangers of mixing legalism and holiness. What makes the rules in Colossians chapter 3 different than a legalistic view of holiness?

DISCOVER
(10 minutes)

Complete the study notes as you watch the DVD together.

The Christian must regularly check _____ to see if it is consistent with Christ.

Being raised with Christ means a change in _____ and _____ or _____.

We change our behavior by changing our _____ life.

Let God transform you into a new person by changing the way you _____.

Actions begin in our _____ life.

The _____ is the father to the deed.

If you sow a thought, you reap an _____; if you sow an action, you reap a _____; and if you sow a habit, you reap a _____.

Christ not only died for our sins, he died _____ sin, breaking its power.

> Paul described in this passage what theologians call our union with Christ. When we place our faith and trust in Jesus, we are united with him in his life, death, and resurrection. His life becomes our life and ours becomes his. When God looks at a believer, he sees someone who is in Christ. There's no better place to be.

Through Christ, we can have _____ over our old sin nature.

Our comfort is in knowing that our life is _____ with Christ and is _____ in his care. Let your _____ and your _____.

If we shed our _____, we must put on _____.

Christianity is a new way of _____, _____, and _____.

It is the Christian's duty to put off (1) _____,
(2) _____, (3) _____, (4) _____,
and (5) _____.

DISCUSS
(25–30 minutes)

1. Why is behavior such an important aspect of the Christian walk?

2. How do your thoughts affect the way you act and react in various circumstances?

3. Why is it so hard to control your thoughts?

4. How can believers "take every thought captive" to the mind of Christ?

5. How does someone "put off" a specific behavior? How does one "put on" the mind of Christ?

Believers have been raised with Christ. Just as he was raised from the dead, so are all Christians delivered from spiritual death—the penalty and power of sin—and raised to new, victorious life in him.

6. What does it mean to be in the world but not of it?

7. How is a Christian truly different from someone who has not experienced new life in Jesus?

8. In what ways does American culture make it difficult to avoid being affected by the five things Christians are supposed to put off?

IMPLEMENT
(5–10 minutes)

Choose at least one activity to do before the next session. Tell one other person which item you chose.

1. Begin each day of the next week by intentionally putting off your old nature and putting on the mind of Christ.

2. Ask a close friend to hold you accountable for your thoughts and behavior in areas where you are struggling.

> *When Paul talked about putting off the old self, he went beyond specific acts to focusing on matters of the heart, such as lust, greed, and anger. These heart issues are the source of evil actions.*

3. Ask the Holy Spirit to examine your heart and reveal to you any struggles or temptations you need to deal with rather than ignore.

4. Discuss with another believer ways you can be in the world but not of it, ways that are specific to your current life situations (such as at work, the gym, etc.).

WRAP UP
(5 minutes)

In the next lesson Pastor Loy will be examining what it means to clothe yourself with the mind of Christ. As you learn to put off the thoughts and behaviors of your old way of life, it is important to discover how Christ wants to renew your mind and fill it with thoughts that will empower you for holy living. Prepare for the next lesson by reading Colossians 3:10–17.

Fresh Holy Clothes

COLOSSIANS 3:10–17

WELCOME and PRAYER
(5 minutes)

SHARE
(10 minutes)

*Take turns sharing what you learned
from applying the last session.*

CONNECT
(15–20 minutes)

William had driven for more than twenty hours by the time he pulled in to the parking lot of the hotel. He looked and smelled as if he had been holed up in the car for a week. His clothes carried the faint scent of fast food. His eyes were red and his hair was a mess. After he checked in, he went directly to his room to shower up and put on a new set of clothes. He came down from his room a truly changed man, and spent the rest of day relaxing by the pool.

Have you ever had to wear the same clothes for more than one or two days? What did it feel like to put on a fresh set of clothes?

Facilitator: Lead the group to participate in the following activity.

Take no more than three minutes to think about and write down your best-guess answers to the following questions:

- How many people in the group have ever had to wear the same clothes more than forty-eight consecutive hours?

- How many people in the group wore more than two sets of clothes yesterday?

- How many people in the group already know specifically what they are going to wear tomorrow?

After three minutes, work as a group to learn the correct answers to the questions.

DISCOVER
(10 minutes)

Complete the study notes as you watch the DVD together.

The new self requires _____.

The new self is not static; it requires a daily _____.

When Paul talks about clothing ourselves, we must understand that he is talking about an _____ transformation.

Jesus _____ people; he had _____ on them; and he _____ their needs.

> Compassion is defined as a feeling of deep sympathy and sorrow for another who is stricken by misfortune, accompanied by a strong desire to alleviate the suffering.

Compassion means "_____."

Compassion sees the _____ of people around them.

_____ is the choice to get involved.

Pride is the opposite of _____.

Humility is not _____ ourselves up, nor is it about denying our _____.

Gentleness is not _____; it is _____ under control.

Patience means _____-tempered.

"Patience is not passive . . . it's _____ strength."
—Bulwer

Forgiveness may be the single most difficult _____, but it is _____.

If we don't learn to forgive, we will become _____ and not _____.

Love is the _____ by which all information is processed.

Love is the _____ for everything.

Love is the strongest _____ in the world.

Let _____ be your highest goal.

God's Word must _____ in us.

We should do all things for God's _____.

We live for an _____ of _____.

DISCUSS
(25–30 minutes)

Patience is the ability to remain calm, focused, and respectful of others when faced with inconveniences, obstacles, delays, difficult people, and other minor or major difficulties.

1. What part does knowledge play in the act of renewing our mind in Christ?

2. Why do you think we need to continually renew our lives and minds to be more like Christ?

3. Pastor Loy linked together compassion and kindness. What is their relationship? Could you have compassion without kindness?

4. Why do you think humility is so important to a changed life?

5. In what ways does patience require strength?

6. Why can forgiveness be so difficult for those who have been forgiven so much already?

7. How is love the greatest attribute?

8. What do the verses in today's lesson teach us about living in Christian community?

9. If peace rules in the hearts of those in Christian community, how should that change peoples' behavior?

IMPLEMENT
(5–10 minutes)

Choose at least one activity to do before the next session. Tell one other person which item you chose.

1. As you get dressed each morning this next week, imagine that you are putting on the fresh clothes of holiness. Dedicate your mind and heart to God as you get ready for your day.

2. Which of the five qualities we are to clothe ourselves with do you wrestle with the most (patience, gentleness, etc.)? Create an action plan for growing in this area.

> *Most modern English dictionaries contain more than twenty variant definitions of love. The love Paul speaks about is the kind of love Christ demonstrated—selfless and sacrificial.*

3. If there is someone you need to forgive or seek forgiveness from, make time to talk with that person this week. Take a friend with you for support if needed.

4. Write or print out Colossians 3:12–14 and keep it with you throughout the next week, reading it regularly. Try to memorize it and let it sink below the surface of your life.

WRAP UP
(5 minutes)

In the next lesson Pastor Loy will be exploring the relationship between husband and wife. Marriage is a wonderful, beautiful, and sometimes fragile flower. In the study passage for next week, Colossians 3:18–25, Paul taught the foundation for a healthy marriage—the foundation of mutual, sacrificial love.

A Love-Filled Marriage

COLOSSIANS 3:18–25

WELCOME and PRAYER
(5 minutes)

SHARE
(10 minutes)

Take turns sharing what you learned from applying the last session.

CONNECT
(15–20 minutes)

Gary wanted to buy a boat, but he knew he shouldn't make such a decision without his wife Sally's input. Unfortunately, when he presented his idea to her, she had strong reservations. Buying a boat would stretch them financially, and with their work schedules, she wondered how often they would actually be able to put a boat in the water. After kindly and respectfully sharing her concern, Sally said she would support whatever decision her husband made. Gary still wanted a boat, but he deeply respected his wife's feelings and opinions. Ultimately, he decided he could wait until Sally was on board with the decision.

The word *submission* stirs up all kinds of negative thoughts and emotions, but the kind of submission Paul advocated is a mutual submission, bathed in kindness, respect, and selfless love.

Facilitator: Lead the group to participate in the following discussion.

Discuss the following questions:

- What examples have you seen of couples who seem to have an outstanding relationship? What do you think is the secret to their success?

- What do you think the Bible has to say about authority in the family and the proper relationship between husband and wife? How do you feel about what you know of its teaching?

DISCOVER
(10 minutes)

Complete the study notes as you watch the DVD together.

The home is at the _____ of God's heart.

Home is the very first _____ that was created.

One of the best things we can do for society is to establish _____ homes.

Prior to Christ, _____ were not recognized as they are today.

Submission simply means to place in an _____ fashion.

Husbands should treat their wives as _____ treats the _____.

> Yielding to another person carries with it the connotation of giving up your rights for the benefit of the other. It is an act of sacrificial love.

The husband has a significant responsibility to _____ his wife.

The word for love, _____, means to sacrifice and to serve.

Headship is not _____, it is _____.

When a marriage is built on the lordship of Jesus Christ, _____ and sacrificial love is always lived out.

In a Harvard study, the divorce rate for couples married in church was one out of _____. For couples married in church, who also attend weekly, read the Bible, and pray together, it was one out of _____.

Children have rights, but more importantly they have
_____.

Children who get along with their parents have far less
_____ in their lives.

Children do not _____ problems as much as they
_____ them.

The Christian should be the best _____ in the place.

DISCUSS
(25–30 minutes)

1. Do you think the Bible gives the husband permission to dominate in the marriage? Why or why not?

> Obedience is defined as complying with or following the commands, restrictions, wishes, or instructions of another with respect and without complaint.

2. Do you think the Bible expects the husband to make every decision in the marriage? Why or why not?

3. How do you think a healthy marriage operates in terms of leadership and submission?

4. How do you think a husband can best honor his wife and help her contribute her unique gifts, understanding, and abilities?

5. How do you think a wife can best assert her own gifts, understanding, and abilities without usurping her husband's leadership?

6. What are some practical ways a husband can love his wife like Christ loves the Church?

Slavery, as Paul spoke of it in the biblical context, has much more in common with the modern-day workforce than it does the oppressive slavery of the eighteenth and nineteenth centuries.

7. What are some practical ways a wife can yield to her husband?

8. How well do you think the church in America is responding to the problem of divorce? How can we do better?

9. In what ways do you think parents are responsible for the behavior of their children? What, if any, are the limits of their responsibility?

IMPLEMENT
(5–10 minutes)

Choose at least one activity to do before the next session. Tell one other person which item you chose.

1. Couples: Take time this week to talk about God's plan for marriage. Discuss what is working well in your marriage relationship and what could work better.

2. Husbands: Examine your life to determine how you can grow closer to the ideal of loving your wife as Christ loved the Church. How can you help your wife become everything God has created her to be?

3. Wives: Evaluate how you are doing with supporting your husband's leadership. What are you doing well already? In what areas might you be able to grow?

4. Parents: Consider ways in which you can better love, care for, support, and encourage your children to grow and mature in their social and spiritual relationships.

WRAP UP
(5 minutes)

In the next lesson, Pastor Loy will explore the vital element of prayer in the life of a Christian. Most Christians understand that prayer is important, but few have the focus and tenacity to develop a healthy, robust prayer life. Read Colossians 4:1–4 this week and commit to praying each day.

A Life of Prayer

COLOSSIANS 4:1–4

WELCOME and PRAYER
(5 minutes)

SHARE
(10 minutes)

*Take turns sharing what you learned
from applying the last session.*

CONNECT
(15–20 minutes)

In the late seventh century, the monks of Southern France constantly sought different ways to remind themselves and others to pray. One day as they prepared bread, they cut the dough in strips and twisted them in a way that resembled a child's arms folded in prayer. They used these pieces of bread as a reminder to pray at mealtime and throughout the day. In the process, they also created a snack that has satisfied people's hunger for more than thirteen centuries: the pretzel.

When the topic of prayer comes up, do you hang your head because you feel guilty about not praying enough? What steps can you take to make prayer a more natural and consistent part of your life?

Facilitator: Lead the group to participate in the following activity.

Share with the group a worry or concern that's on your heart today. Then take time to pray as a group for all the concerns. Your group may choose to pray silently, pray out loud as group members feel prompted, or one or two volunteers might lead the entire group in prayer.

DISCOVER
(10 minutes)

Complete the study notes as you watch the DVD together.

_____ is the great privilege that the Christian has been given.

It is only through prayer that the _____ of God can truly be seen.

Our prayer must be _____.

Prayer is the _____ of our souls.

Prayer is not to be _____ and half-hearted, but with _____ and _____.

Relentless prayer _____ priority.

Prayer is the _____ thing a Christian can do. Prayer is the _____ by which we build effectiveness.

Relentless prayer insists _____. Meaningless _____ develop _____ living.

Relentless prayer involves _____. Time develops _____, and familiarity develops _____.

Relentless prayer invites _____. We should always expect _____ from God, because that's the kind of God we serve.

> Do not be anxious about anything, but in everything, by prayer and petition, with thanksgiving, present your requests to God (Phil. 4:6).

Our praying must be _____. Our prayers should be _____ like a skilled archer.

Our praying must be with _____. _____ is a key indicator of true and authentic faith.

Our praying must be _____. Paul says to pray for _____.

God's Word never returns _____.

Prayer activates the _____ of God through the mouth of man.

DISCUSS
(25–30 minutes)

1. Why is prayer so important to the Christian life?

2. What are some practical ways that have helped you make prayer a priority in your life?

3. Jesus said that if we believe, we will be given whatever we ask for in prayer. Why do you think we don't always receive things we have prayed for?

> Prayer is a privilege and one of the most vital components of the Christian life. It is our primary opportunity to communicate with God. Without it, there is no relationship.

4. How can we make our prayers more focused? What is the benefit of a focused prayer?

5. How does gratitude in our prayers show that our faith is genuine and authentic?

6. Are there items or requests that are not appropriate to mention in prayer? If so, what are they?

7. How can a person learn to pray? What has helped you learn to pray?

8. Discuss what Paul meant by praying without ceasing.

IMPLEMENT
(5–10 minutes)

Choose at least one activity to do before the next session. Tell one other person which item you chose.

1. Create a physical reminder to help you remember to pray multiple times throughout the day. It could be a rubber band around your wrist or a 3 x 5 card in your car.

> *Several studies show that the average Christian prays for about one minute per day.*

2. Establish regular times for prayer each day. You might pray in the morning when you first wake up, at lunchtime, and in the evening just before you go to sleep.

3. Maintain a current prayer list. Don't forget to include standard or regular prayer requests, like praying for your spouse and kids. Keep your list somewhere prominent, so you will see it often.

4. Tell a friend that you are making an effort to strengthen your prayer life. Ask him or her to keep you accountable by asking about your efforts on a weekly basis.

WRAP UP
(5 minutes)

In the next lesson Pastor Loy will explore the necessity of accessing God's wisdom in our daily lives. Too often we rely on our own strength and ability to solve problems. Above all, we need God's wisdom when facing everyday life situations. Check out Colossians 4:5 before next week.

Be Wise in Conduct

COLOSSIANS 4:5

WELCOME and PRAYER
(5 minutes)

SHARE
(10 minutes)

Take turns sharing what you learned from applying the last session.

CONNECT
(15–20 minutes)

The "Hoosier Poet" James Whitcomb Riley, known for his keen sense of humor and insight, once said, "When I see a bird that walks like a duck and swims like a duck and quacks like a duck, I call that bird a duck." Behavior is one of the only indicators of the character of a person. If a person harbors bitterness and often lashes out in anger, then that person is most likely an angry person, whether or not he or she admits it.

What do your actions say about you? Are your actions different than the words you use to describe yourself?

Facilitator: Lead the group to participate in the following activity.

Play a brief game of charades as a group. The topics can be whatever the group chooses. The point of this game is for the group to notice how our actions give clues that help people watching know who or what we are. Discuss this concept before moving into the DVD portion of the lesson.

DISCOVER
(10 minutes)

Complete the study notes as you watch the DVD together.

Our _____ behavior is the best offense we have.

Our _____ as Christians is the greatest evidence we have of the gospel of Christ.

Our actions will either _____ Christ, or degrade the cross.

"_____ is the perpetual revealing of us."
—F. D. Huntington

Colossians 4:5

Conduct yourselves with _____. Our conduct is the proof in _____ and _____ we believe.

_____ is living right in the face of any condition.

Christians are to be _____, but not _____. It doesn't mean we have to _____ to _____.

The righteous lifestyle is a _____ that draws.

_____ among Christians is rampant. _____ and _____ have become a booming industry inside the church. _____, _____, and _____ are out of control.

Make the most of the _____.

God doesn't need our witness tomorrow; he needs it _____.

Keep your _____ excellent among the Gentiles, so that they may see your good deeds and glorify God.

Wisdom is about the application of knowledge, discernment, and insight—knowledge of what is true or right coupled with the ability to make sound and just decisions about what action to take.

"I will govern my life and my thoughts as if the whole world were to _____ the one, and to _____ the other."

—Seneca

71

Our behavior speaks volumes about _____ we really are.

Behavior is the _____ in which everyone displays his image.

DISCUSS
(25–30 minutes)

1. In what ways is wisdom different than knowledge?

> And we are instructed to turn from godless living and sinful pleasures. We should live in this evil world with wisdom, righteousness, and devotion to God (Titus 2:12 NLT).

2. Why does a person's behavior speak louder than his or her words?

3. How does our conduct affect our witness with those we work and live with?

4. Discuss the meaning of the saying "Witness at all times and if needed, use words."

5. What types of behaviors are the best witnesses for non-Christians?

6. Even deeper than conduct, what type of a heart does Jesus desire us to have?

7. How does having a heart for Jesus affect our conduct?

8. Can someone have bad behavior but a good heart? Why or why not?

9. What would it look like for our behavior to reflect the image of God?

IMPLEMENT
(5–10 minutes)

Choose at least one activity to do before the next session. Tell one other person which item you chose.

1. Make it a point to pay careful attention to your behavior in the upcoming week. Ask the Holy Spirit to reveal to you any behavior that reflects negatively on Christ.

   > "Let your light shine before men," Jesus said, "in such a way that they may see your good works, and glorify your Father who is in heaven" (Matt. 5:16 NASB).

2. As you pay attention to your behavior, note any actions that create friction or other kinds of tension in your relationships with others. Consider how you might change those behaviors and strengthen healthy relationships.

3. Consider ways in which your actions can be a silent witness to people at work or in your neighborhood who don't know Christ. Identify ways in which small changes in behavior could make a big difference in the way people perceive your witness.

4. Pray for those around you who don't know Christ and for the opportunity to be a witness to them.

WRAP UP
(5 minutes)

In the final lesson of our study, Pastor Loy focuses on how our conversations with others can either encourage people or tear them down. Negative talk, gossip, and coarse joking are easy traps to fall into, even in the church. Guard your heart this week against falling for these. Study Colossians 4:6–18 for next lesson.

May Your Words Be Salt

WELCOME and PRAYER
(5 minutes)

SHARE
(10 minutes)

*Take turns sharing what you learned
from applying the last session.*

CONNECT
(15–20 minutes)

In *The Message* version of the Bible, Eugene Peterson translated Proverbs 18:21 this way: "Words kill, words give life; they're either poison or fruit—you choose." Words have the power of life and death. Maybe you remember a time when someone you loved said something that hurt you and how much their words stung. Or perhaps you remember the last time someone paid you a meaningful compliment and what a boost it was to your confidence and self-esteem.

Consider how your words affect others. Do your words salt or sour your conversations? Do your words and your actions line up as they should?

Facilitator: Lead the group to participate in the following discussion.

Discuss as a group why it is that so many prominent pastors have experienced moral failure. They can serve as case studies on what happens when words and deeds don't match up. How do you think the failures of these public figures affect the way the world views all Christians?

DISCOVER
(10 minutes)

Complete the study notes as you watch the DVD together.

Our _____ have little value without a lifestyle to match.

Our _____ and our _____ must be in harmony with one another.

It is not enough to _____ wisely among unbelievers; we must _____ with them as well.

Our speech should be as _____ spoke, with _____.

Our words should always profess _____ to those who hear, but they cannot do that unless we have grace in our _____.

In Paul's day, salt was not only used as a preservative but for _____ as well.

Our speech should not be such that it could be taken _____, but flavored that it would provide a healthy _____.

> If anyone considers himself religious and yet does not keep a tight rein on his tongue, he deceives himself and his religion is worthless (James 1:26).

Salt was also used for _____. When Paul tells us to offer our _____ as a sacrifice, our _____ are to be included.

Too often, one's _____ and one's _____ contradict.

Three common double talks are (1) _____, (2) _____, and (3) _____.

Every _____ should be carefully crafted for the _____ up and never for the _____ down.

"_____ is a personal confession either of malice or stupidity."

—J. G. Holland

The writer of Proverbs tells us that there are six things that God hates, and one of them is a _____.

"When _____, _____, and _____ are all working together, it makes for a powerful _____."

—Warren Wiersbe

DISCUSS
(25–30 minutes)

1. Consider a time when the speech of someone you held in high regard didn't match his or her actions. How did that affect your perception of that person?

> The tongue also is a fire, a world of evil among the parts of the body. It corrupts the whole person, sets the whole course of his life on fire, and is itself set on fire by hell (James 3:6).

2. Why do you think Christians often fall into the trap of having contradicting words and actions?

3. Discuss Paul's use of salt as an analogy for our speech. Why do you think he chose that analogy?

4. Why do you suppose gossip is a common temptation and pitfall for many Christians? What can help Christians to avoid this temptation?

5. What should you do if you realize you have been guilty of passing on wrong information, either intentionally or unintentionally?

6. In Matthew 12:34, Jesus said, "For out of the overflow of the heart the mouth speaks." Discuss the meaning of Jesus' statement.

7. Paul told us to let our conversation always be full of grace. How would our conversations look if they were always full of grace? How would they be different?

> Do not let any unwholesome talk come out of your mouths, but only what is helpful for building others up according to their needs, that it may benefit those who listen (Eph. 4:29).

8. What are some practical ways we can align our speech and our deeds so that they both reflect God's heart?

IMPLEMENT
(5–10 minutes)

Choose at least one activity to do before the next session. Tell one other person which item you chose.

1. Ask a friend or spouse to honestly grade whether your words and your deeds match each other, or if they contradict. Be prepared to receive the feedback, and respond with grace.

2. Discuss with other believers what constitutes foul language or coarse joking. Think outside of your own culture and language to matters of heart and intention.

3. Make a point to have intentional but casual conversations that are laced with salt with non-Christians in your community.

4. Memorize Ephesians 4:29 this week.

WRAP UP
(5 minutes)

Colossians is a key text for believers. By studying it together we've acknowledged the supremacy of Christ over all creation, discovered our true identity in Christ, and learned to walk in freedom and holiness through the power of Christ.

Also in the Celebrate Series—*Celebrate James.*